The Monkey Season

Robertas Aleksandravicius

BookLeaf Publishing

India | USA | UK

Presentation by *BookLeaf Publishing*

Web: www.bookleafpub.com

E-mail: info@bookleafpub.com

ISBN: 978-93-5744-734-8

First edition 2022

DEDICATION

To my most faithful friend.

ACKNOWLEDGEMENT

I want to thank my wife, Vicky. You encouraged me to write this. You are my greatest supporter. I love you.

PREFACE

These poems are my life. I was writing them during a challenging season. There were so many questions and very few answers. These poems are the monkeys that have taken over my head. They jump around, they destroy things, they love me: and I love them. Even when they are confusing and frustrating, they are my monkeys.

Monkeys

Monkeys
Loud, destructive
Jeering, stomping, hanging
They are my thoughts
Wild

Worries

Sleepless nights with you.
Terrified of the future.
Am I lost or found?

Auburn thoughts

A rapid serpent,
A slug crossing autumn paths,
How hard is silence?

Soul seasons

A year is four-part. (some places)
Souls are more complicated.
There are a thousand moments in every hour of
every day.
We organize them into thick, lined books.
The rules are firm.
Procedures have to be followed, but they won't
abide.
So we stress and sweat, self-medicate and panic.
We google for abnormalities.
We diagnose, but really, they are a thousand
breaths of a life well-lived.
All different, all precious.
All misunderstood.

Fog

So dark
And frightening
The fog surrounding me
Will I entrust my shaking hands
To you?

Numbers

Four leaves - on the ground.
Two colours -yellow and red.
One soul - searching for peace.

Evil words

Why is it that the rhyming comes so hard?
It's like the words have grievances with me.
All my attempts the devils disregard,
Should I give up and offer them some tea?

Wife

Wife
Tired, worried
Running, learning, fighting
She cares a lot
Companion

Mastery

So far,
my purpose I have understood.
But here it is again:
Horizon new.
Repeat.

Attempting solitude

Thoughts come like waves,
Their wet, little hands hold my brain underwater,
Until I gasp for relief from their oppression.
They let go, ever so slightly, only to return a
minute later.

My life is a boat in danger of destruction.
I do, however, have an anchor.
I rarely use it. I am not exactly sure why that is.
Maybe I am afraid of being bound?

The deck is creaking.
In this case, captivity is freedom.
My anchor is a Name, the Name is Peace.
He does not remove the storm, but he holds me
steady.

Peace and security

Peace and security, our minds they dull.
Wealth and prosperity, to sleep they lull.
How can we sober and alert remain,
When all that we are taught is "watch and play"?
Look down, they say, you mind your business,
now,
This tweet, please like, this tragedy lament.
But now move on, is not this kitten cute?
What was it that we spoke about? Oh dear!
Our memories are frail, our hearts cement.
Humanity surrendered to machines.

Community

My conclusion on the case of community,
Is that (oh darn, it's devastating),
I'd rather choose to champion my perspective,
Because (oh holy hat, it's hard),
To lay down self.

Psalm 42
(re-imagined)

I need you. I am tired and frustrated.
Where are you?
I remember the good times we had with a smile
and pain in my heart.
Why am I in this state when you are embracing
me?

I am tormented by dark thoughts,
So I try to focus on you.
But it feels like I'm drowning.
I'm overwhelmed.

I fluctuate between hope and despair.
But I know that you are there for me during the
day,
And you never stop watching me even during
the night.

Have you forgotten me?
I'm tempted to start listening to other people:
They say that you don't care about me.

Why am I in this state?
Why am I tortured?

Still, I will hope for better days,
And trust that your love will hold me.

Still

15

Sometimes
The greatest victory
Over myself
Is to do nothing.

Marriage

Prison. Elegantly crafted air-bars.
Mind patterns. Decisions made in the state of
love. Or was it fear?
A firm resolve to endure careful observation.
Caring confusion, words unspoken, feelings
written on walls with lifeforce.
A mountain of hurt, rivers disappointments. Joy.
The bird remains. Is it wisdom or foolishness?

I am an adult

"I am an adult" - I say. So proud.
I have moved on from childish things.
I have toiled and I've deserved to learn no more.
I'm being forced to learn again.

It wounds my pride, this I admit.
It hurts my sense of self-efficacy.
It makes me ask uncomfortable questions about
myself.
It pulls me off my self-made pedestal.

But it is good for me, I have to say.
But it makes me more gracious with others.
But it helps me be a whole person.
But it is easier to breathe as a child.

Confusion

If only I could have clarity of mind,
that poets write about - alas.
Confusion, concussion. Teeth shattering on a
rock.
My thoughts are buzzing as a massive beehive.
Stones crushing through the roof.
Conundrums drumming in the back of my skull.
Weirdness.

Peace

What is peace?
Is it a state? A place? A condition?
Trust in the mad driver in the dark tunnel?
How I desire peace.
A state. A place. A condition.
Trust in the good driver in the dark tunnel.

Friend

Just take a breath, feel the water
Even as your eyes are blind to the beauty
Still, hands that shaped anemones
Untie the knots of your resistance
Songs fill your cells